DI000697

Gambling

WITHDRAWN

GAMBLING

Winners

&
Losers

Margaret O. Hyde

THE MILLBROOK PRESS
BROOKFIELD, CONNECTICUT

NEWTON COUNTY LIBRARY
1174 MONTICELLO STREET
COVINGTON, GA

Library of Congress Cataloging-in-Publication Data
Hyde, Margaret O. (Margaret Oldroyd), 1917–
Gambling: winners and losers / by Margaret O. Hyde
p.   cm.
Includes bibliographical references (p.   ) and index.
Summary: Addresses the issues of legalized gambling, illegal
gambling, and compulsive gambling in an even-handed way.
ISBN 1-56294-532-7
1. Gambling—United States—Juvenile literature.   I. Title.
HV6715.H93   1995   363.4'2'0973—dc 20   94-46874   CIP   AC

Photographs courtesy of UPI/Bettmann: p. 11; Rothco Cartoons: pp. 14
(Linda Boileau, *Frankfort State Journal*, Ky.), 32 (*Punch*), 63, 76 (Dick
Adair, *Honolulu Advertiser*); The Liaison Network: pp. 18 (© Michael
Springer), 28 (© Alain Benainous), 35 (© David Kampfner), 38 (©
Neal Palumb), 54 (© Randy Taylor), 70 (© Alain Benainous), 78
(© Steve Allen); The Bettmann Archive: pp. 21, 25; New Jersey
Newsphotos: p. 30; Wide World Photos: pp. 46, 65, 67.

Published by The Millbrook Press
2 Old New Milford Road, Brookfield, Connecticut 06804

Copyright © 1995 by Margaret O. Hyde
All rights reserved
Printed in the United States of America
1 3 5 4 2

Contents

Gambling

Chapter One

Gambling: Fun or Trouble?

America is experiencing a gambling boom. Legal gambling is becoming a national passion, while illegal gambling continues to thrive. Teens have joined the gambling fever in greater numbers than ever before, even though laws forbid most of them to wager. Studies show that about half of the high school students in states where gambling is legal have probably gambled for money in the last month. While estimates vary, as many as 8 percent of teenagers appear to have serious problems that are gambling related.[1]

Each toss of the dice, sports bet, lottery ticket, and blackjack game can make people feel special and lucky. Win or lose, gamblers of all ages take risks, experience excitement, and, in most cases, have fun.

For some people, gambling makes life better; for others it is an all-consuming addiction that makes life worse. For the majority of gamblers it is recreation, but for some it is a serious disease. Strong opinions exist about gambling, with good arguments for and against it.

In addition to more lotteries, illegal sports betting, bingo, and other games of chance, casino gambling is spreading across the country. By 1994, riverboat casinos legally provided games of chance on the waters of Illinois, Iowa, Louisiana, Mississippi, and Missouri, and dozens more states were considering making it legal for casinos to float on their rivers. Riverboat gambling and other casino operations are not always financially successful, however. States frequently overestimate the revenue that will come from legalized gambling, although some of these ventures pay off in the early days. For this as well as other reasons, the controversy continues.[2]

American Indian-run casinos have multiplied, with a number of reservations making huge amounts of money. The sounds of roulette wheels, video poker, slot machines, and other games of chance are ringing in a new era for numerous American Indian tribes.[3] With their winnings, some tribes have been able to afford new homes, businesses, schools, health-care centers, community centers, and other much-needed help. Tribal gambling appears to be relatively free of crime, but do increased opportunities to gamble increase the danger of crime or of addiction to gambling?

Lottery fever—in the 1993 to 1994 fiscal
year, $2.37 billion were spent on games
sponsored by the New York State Lottery
Commission. Forty-two percent, $1.1 billion,
was earmarked for education.

GAMBLING BOOM IN AMERICA: PROS AND CONS

Gambling has become one of the fastest-growing industries in the United States. From New Hampshire's first lottery in 1964 to today's new theme parks at many casinos, the gambling industry has taken on a new image as entertainment. At some casinos, families are encouraged to bring their children, and activities are provided for the young while parents take their chances.

Whether or not the revised description of gambling at casinos as "family entertainment" sends the wrong message to young people is a topic for debate. Bingo has long been a part of the casino nights held by some houses of worship, although others disapprove of all forms of gambling. A Saturday night poker game for high stakes or pennies may be a family ritual.

There are also moral and ethical issues involved on which people disagree. Is it wrong to gamble? Is it unethical to encourage people to spend money on games that they don't have much chance of winning? Should states promote lotteries if they know there are people who may become addicted to gambling?

The title of the Afterword in *Temples of Chance*, a book about commercial gambling, is "Coming Soon to a Neighborhood Near You." The author, David Johnston, begins this section by predicting that almost every place in America where gambling has not already arrived will soon join the trend. On the other hand, Nelson Rose, a gambling expert and professor at the Whittier Law School in Los Angeles, California, predicts that all gambling will be outlawed in about thirty-five years as the result of a moral backlash.[4]

People also disagree on which games of chance cause the greatest problem with addiction. For example, video games are considered more addicting than table games because they are fast-moving. In a video game, there is less time between the movements or choices the players make and the outcome—win or lose—than in games whose playing times depend on the speed of the dealer who hands out cards around the table.[5]

Societies have tried to control gambling since ancient times on the grounds that it encourages idleness and crime. The long-term connection between gambling and illegal activities is well known. Early private lotteries were banned in the United States because of corruption and fraud. The syndicates that ran numbers games and offtrack horse betting often established ties with local politicians and took over political organizations.[6] The links between legal and illegal gambling and crime figures have always been well publicized.

Government lotteries take in about $25 billion a year.[7] With so much money to be earned, it is likely that opportunities to gamble will continue to increase.

GAMBLING: HARMLESS ENTERTAINMENT?

Suppose you had to vote on whether to allow gambling in your state. Do you know enough about it to make a wise decision? Is government-sponsored gambling actually a "regressive tax," for which low-

As this cartoon shows, the get-rich-quick
fantasies of gambling for those who can't afford it
may lead to disaster. Dorothy, the character from *The
Wizard of Oz*, is dancing along the yellow brick road,
totally unaware of the dangers ahead.

income persons pay proportionately more of their
income than high-income persons? Are the millions
of low-income lottery players aware of the small
chance they have of winning? Do they care? Cer-
tainly, lottery advertising does not stress that the
chances of losing are tremendously higher than the
chances of winning. Should people be prevented
from gambling for fun if they can afford it and keep it
under control?

With the exception of Utah and Hawaii, it is now legal to place a bet of some kind anywhere in the United States.[8] Americans wagered more than $300 billion per year in the early 1990s.[9] This figure does not include the amount of money involved in illegal gambling, such as betting on college and professional sports. Some gambling experts estimate that the amount of money bet in illegal gambling could be from $30 billion to $200 billion a year.[10] The profits of the gambling industry are difficult to estimate, since so much of it is illegal, but there is no question that they are huge.

Today, gambling competes with the film and video industries for entertainment dollars. It equals, or even surpasses, them in some states. According to Martin Christiansen, who tracks gambling growth for the *International Gaming and Wagering Business* magazine, the percentage of personal income spent on gambling in one year is comparable to what Americans spend on dentistry, health clubs, or beauty parlors.[11]

Even though it is illegal for teens to gamble, they do gamble among themselves, and some gain access to commercial games. Teen gambling is one of the reasons some people believe gambling should not be legalized and is of great concern to gambling establishments, which can be fined heavily for admitting people who are underage. For a small percentage of teens, gambling can be the beginning of serious problems.

People's reasons for gambling differ. Most enjoy the entertainment and the hope of winning money.

Many gamblers like the feelings of romance, euphoria, self-importance, and intoxication. The losses are accepted as part of the risk of this form of entertainment.

The gambling impulse appeals to what has been called the adventurer in us, the part that seeks to experience change, the unknown, chance, danger, and all that is new.[12] A person's fear of danger, voluntary exposure to it, and the hope that all will turn out well are part of many activities, such as auto racing, skiing, flying, rock climbing, white-water rafting, or traveling to unknown lands. The risk of losing can make a game of chance exciting to some people. Gambling has been called a way of "buying hope on credit."

Who really wins and who really loses in today's gambling boom? For most people gambling is a form of recreation, for others it can become a serious problem. Compulsive gambling has been called a silent disease. It is easy to hide, especially in the early stages. Many gamblers find it hard to say when gambling for them changed from a social activity to an addiction.

It is more than luck that determines the true winners and losers in gambling. In your adult life, you will need to make decisions about gambling. If you choose to gamble, you will also need to understand the potential dangers.

Chapter Two

Gambling: The World's Oldest Recreation

Picture two prehistoric hunters wagering on the possibility of finding a bear in a cave they are exploring. One bets that at least one bear will be there; the second bets that the cave is empty. One wagers his tools, but the other likes to take big risks, so he bets his food and his dwelling. Number one is not going to be outdone, so he bets his food and dwelling too.

No one knows whether cavemen bet this way, but archaeologists think it is a good possibility that gambling began long before recorded history.[1] It is believed that horse racing existed in very ancient times.[2]

No one knows when people began to bet on camel races in Turkey, bullfights in Spain, tortoise races in Thailand, or scorpion matches in Arab countries. An endless number of animal races were attracting gamblers very long ago. Fantan, a game in which beans are counted and bets are placed on the number of beans in a final grouping, was played in China centuries ago. Mah-Jongg is an ancient Chi-

**Mah-Jongg, a game played with tiles engraved
with Chinese drawings and symbols, is one
of the oldest gambling games.**

nese gambling game that is still played in many
communities around the world. The tiles, once made
from bone or ivory, are now plastic, but the game is
the same.

The ancient Egyptians played with a form of
dice that they made from animal bones and shaped
into many-sided pieces about the size of golf balls.
When the tombs of Egyptian pharaohs were un-
earthed, dice and other gambling devices were

found with them.[3] Egyptians buried many articles with the body for the person to use in the afterlife. Gambling was considered a form of entertainment for the hereafter.

Gambling with dice appears to be almost universal. Their first use was probably to interpret dreams and to predict the future.[4] Dice were the gambler's main tool until playing cards appeared during the fourteenth century.[5]

Even the ancient Greek gods were thought to play with dice. In Greek mythology, the gods were said to have rolled dice in order to divide the universe among themselves. Zeus won the earth, Poseidon the sea, and Hades the underworld.[6]

Rulers in the ancient country of Lydia in Asia Minor are believed to have given dice to their citizens during a famine to take their minds off their hunger.[7] Early American Indians played a game in which peach stones were adapted to use as dice.

There are examples in the Bible of events that were determined by casting lots, in the belief that God would control the results.[8] In the Book of Jonah 1:7, lots are cast to determine which man God has chosen: "And they said everyone to his fellow, 'Come, let us cast lots, and the lot fell upon Jonah.' "[9]

Casinos, places where games are played for money, probably existed 1,500 years before the time of Christ. Because springs and good fortune have long been associated, it is not surprising to find that ancient watering holes were popular places for gambling even before the days of the Roman Empire.

The sick, who sought curative waters at spas, also might have sought good fortune with games of chance at the spas. Gambling became so wild at some of these places that officials sought to control it by levying a tax on the revenues from the spas and the gambling done there.[10]

GAMBLING: THE FALL OF THE ROMAN EMPIRE?

The early Romans had a passion for gambling. Archaeologists have found gambling tables scratched on numerous flat surfaces, including the steps of ancient temples, the Forum, and the corridors of the Coliseum.[11] Schoolboys in ancient Rome and Pompeii played a game called "par impar," in which they guessed the number of nuts or beans held in a fist.

The emperor Caligula, famous for his bad deeds, liked to wager with money from the Roman treasury. He also seized the property of wealthy citizens to support his gambling habit. His successor, Claudius, also used money from the public treasury.[12] He had the interior of his carriage built so that he could play dice while traveling. He is believed to have gambled on the day of his sister's funeral and to have wagered the equivalent of $50,000 on one roll of the dice.

One of the most popular types of gambling in ancient Rome was betting on chariot races, and the emperor Nero was said to be addicted to it. It is reported that when his wife scolded him for coming

The most famous scene in the movie classic *Ben-Hur* is the chariot race. This form of racing was popular thousands of years before the Romans staged their racing spectacles.

home late from gambling on his favorite sport, he kicked her so violently he caused her death.[13]

Some historians believe that gambling played a part in the fall of the Roman Empire. Throughout history, wars have been lost and kingdoms have fallen as the heads of countries indulged their gambling fever. In France, during the reign of King Charles V, the Prince of Orange gambled away the money that was entrusted to him to pay the army.[14]

Organized weekly racing goes back to the 12th century, during the reign of Henry II of England.

King Henry VIII, well known for his enormous appetites, had a passion for gambling. He especially liked playing with dice, and a story is told that once he bet the bells of St. Paul's Cathedral against £100 on one roll of the dice. The king lost. The winner collected. The bells had to be broken to get them out of the tower, and the pieces of metal were probably sold as scrap. When the king decided that gambling was a social ill, he instructed the English Parliament in 1541 to pass the Unlawful Games Act, but exempted "gentlemen." This act was not officially rescinded until 1960, but it probably did not curb the gambling of the ordinary people for whom it was intended.[15]

Charles II (1616–1685) was such an avid patron of horse racing that he came to be known as the father of the British turf.[16]

Throughout history, governments have used gambling to raise money. Augustus Caesar sponsored the first known public lottery in order to raise money to repair the city of Rome.[17] L'École Militaire, a French military school that still exists, was founded when King Louis XV of France let the famous adventurer Casanova start a government lottery in the eighteenth century.

THE FOUNDING OF AMERICA FUNDED BY A LOTTERY

In the thirteen colonies, many lotteries operated before the American Revolution as popular ways to raise funds.[18] Even the British colonization of America was financed partly by a lottery that was authorized by James I in 1612. It supplied money for the Virginia Company, which was sending settlers to the New World.

In 1748 a lottery was organized by young Ben Franklin and other prominent citizens to defend Philadelphia from attacks by French soldiers and by Indian tribes. Two other famous lotteries of colonial days include one that John Hancock helped to manage in 1762 to raise money to rebuild Faneuil Hall in Boston after a fire. George Washington managed a lottery to help build a road over the Cumberland Mountains.[19]

Lotteries were popular and considered quite respectable. They helped to establish several prestigious colleges such as Yale, Harvard, Columbia, Dartmouth, and Princeton.

Cardplaying was also popular, and nearly every well-furnished house had a card table. Though George Washington gambled in private life, he objected to gambling among his troops. However, his order banning them from playing cards and other games of chance was widely ignored.[20]

Horse racing, too, was popular. The first American racetrack, the Newmarket, was established in 1665 on Hempstead Plain, Long Island, not far from the present location of the Belmont Park racetrack.[21] Some of the first races were probably held on the main streets of early settlements. Race Street in Philadelphia still bears the name of the course.

In the nineteenth century, gambling in America continued in many forms. Over two thousand river-boat gamblers traveled on American waterways. Professional gamblers preyed on gullible, wealthy passengers.[22]

These professional gamblers cheated so blatantly that gambling was eventually forbidden on the boats. As a result, the number of gambling casinos in many cities multiplied. Many riverfront areas offered cockfights, horse racing, and casino games to those who visited their ports.

OUTLAWING AND REFORM EFFORTS FAIL

Attempts to curtail gambling coincided with the popular reform movements of the nineteenth century. Among the organizations that opposed tobacco, alcohol, slavery, and profanity was one that fought gambling, especially corrupt lotteries. Fraud was common in lottery operations during the 1800s.[23] However, illegal betting continued. In many cities, politicians and police turned "a blind eye" toward gambling because they shared in the profits.[24]

The opening of the "Wild West" gave gambling new life. Gambling was the primary amusement for everyone in frontier towns. Gamblers set up games in tents, in the saloons, and on the streets. The taming of the West and the California Gold Rush are said to have taken place to the sound of the rattle of dice on saloon bars.

Gold miners were often relieved of their gold nuggets by cheaters who mastered a variety of tricks.

Gambling was once more the target of reformers in the late nineteenth century. The Louisiana Lottery was famous for its corruption. It managed to operate despite federal prohibitions because enforcement officials would not prosecute lottery managers. Tickets were sold by mail, and at one time more than 90 percent of the lottery revenue came from out of state. In 1890 the United States Congress passed laws banning the delivery of mail containing items that dealt with lotteries, and the Louisiana Lottery Company moved to Honduras in Central America. Further postal laws eventually put the company out of business. Lotteries then became illegal in the United States from 1895 to 1963.[25]

Slot machines were introduced in the 1890s. Although illegal, their use spread. Early in the 1900s, offtrack betting took place largely in betting shops, but the telephone later became the popular way to make bets, even though laws prohibited the use of the phone for these purposes.

When the twentieth century began, it was generally believed that gambling and crime were closely connected. Anti-gambling laws were only effective when the police, politicians, and the public all cared to enforce them.[26]

Gambling continues to create problems, but public attitudes toward it have become more relaxed. Some people accept gambling as a harmless activity that just needs some controls, and many substitute the word "gaming" for gambling because gaming has a less negative connotation. Others continue to oppose gambling for religious, psychological, financial, or moral reasons.[27]

As the association of gambling with crime or immorality fades, as many as 40 percent of American households may be participating in some form of gambling by the year 2000.[28] As always, a few may be winners, but many will be losers.

Chapter Three

Legalized Gambling in America Today

Although much gambling is still conducted outside the law, the amount of legalized gambling is so great that it is one of the fastest-growing industries in the United States.[1]

GAMBLING IN THE DESERT AND BY THE SEA

When many people think of legalized gambling, they think of Las Vegas, Nevada. The city as a gambling mecca began as the dream of a well-known organized-crime figure, Benjamin (Bugsy) Siegel. According to one account, he was sent to Las Vegas to protect "mob" investments relating to horse bets.[2] According to another account, he sold the casino idea to skeptical members of the mob, and built a glittering palace, the Flamingo, with a bankroll of

Nevada legalized gambling in 1931. The first big gambling casino opened in Las Vegas in 1946. The city and its casinos now attract more than 13 million visitors annually.

millions gained from "bootlegging" illegal alcohol during Prohibition. He was shot by members of the mob in 1947, about a year after his dream came true.[3]

Bugsy Siegel was replaced by Gus Greenbaum, formerly an old friend and a fellow mobster. Greenbaum expanded Las Vegas, building more casinos in moderately priced hotels, roads, and an airport, while contributing generously to municipal authorities, charity organizations, and the police department. Las Vegas is reported to have amassed $4 million in profit in 1950.[4]

Las Vegas had several luxurious hotels and casinos as early as 1932. In the 1940s new resort hotels opened along the main highway to Los Angeles. This section of the road became known as "The Strip." The fact that there was a criminal connection seemed to add excitement for many visitors to what came to be called "Sin City."

Today, casinos try to gain new customers by emphasizing mass entertainment for the entire family. The Land of Oz, pirates, Egyptian settings, and medieval fairs are among the many elaborate themes that are combined with the gambling attractions.

Other important, legal gambling centers in Nevada, such as Reno, Laughlin, and Lake Tahoe, draw much smaller crowds. At Lake Tahoe, one can ski during the day and gamble at night. All of Nevada is open territory for licensed casinos and other gambling centers.[5]

In 1976, after ten years of debate, voters in New Jersey approved a constitutional amendment to introduce casino gambling in Atlantic City. Promoters convinced the people of New Jersey that gambling would revitalize this declining city by the sea. Once a famous and family-oriented resort town, Atlantic City had fallen on hard times. Voters hoped to rescue it through casinos to provide jobs, increase tax reve-

**Although annually more tourists visit
Atlantic City than Las Vegas, many of them
come just for the day on special charter
buses subsidized by the casinos.**

nues, bring visitors to conventions, stimulate the
housing industry, and provide assistance for the dis-
abled and elderly. All funds raised from the licensing
and taxation of gambling operations were to be used
for state and local social programs.[6]

The rejuvenation of Atlantic City did not take place as planned, and results were disappointing a decade into the project. Tourists flocked to the casinos from nearby states, but many of the casinos continued to lose money. The city around the casinos remained a shambles—one block away from the boardwalk with its glamour and tinsel-like trappings were burned-out, boarded-up shops and homes.

New plans to revitalize the city and save the casinos met with skepticism. Some claimed the new programs were too little, too late, while others continued to believe in a brighter future. In the spring of 1994, with the number of visitors continuing to decline, planners worked toward making Atlantic City a tourist destination for the family instead of just a gambling destination for adults. They hoped to attract visitors to conventions and seashore pleasures as well as gambling casinos.[7]

New Orleans, Louisiana, has been famous for its illegal gambling. In the 1990s, with governmental approval for the building of the world's largest casino, The Grand Palais, there was hope of increased revenues for the city. Opponents, however, questioned whether the new casino would solve any problems. Though millions of dollars could be generated in tax revenues and casino jobs created, the benefits for businesses and residents had not materialized in many communities where gambling had been made legal.

Smaller casinos have sprung up in other areas, such as Central City, Colorado, a former mining town where most of the original buildings have been gutted, but the atmosphere of the Old West remains. The average Colorado betting room has three blackjack tables, a poker table, and only forty slot machines. In Deadwood, South Dakota, slot machines whir in hotel lobbies, and gamblers play their games in about eighty licensed gambling houses.

When gamblers in casinos are listening to the sounds of coins falling into buckets and the screams of excited "winners," they may forget that the biggest winner of all is always the casino.

"It's the gamble I like about owning a casino . . . some days you win, some days you win more."

GAMBLING ON
AMERICAN INDIAN RESERVATIONS

Gambling has brought prosperity to many American Indian tribes in recent years. The rights of American Indians to operate casinos were confirmed by the Indian Gaming Regulatory Act in 1988. The law requires a "compact" between a tribe and state officials, setting rules for the enterprise. State laws that restrict gambling don't apply to American Indian reservations because American Indians have a measure of sovereignty over those lands. In spite of considerable debates with states over such matters as land ownership, zoning laws, and increased traffic problems, the number of casinos on reservations continues to increase.

The Mashantucket Pequot Indians run Foxwoods High Stakes Bingo and Casino, near Ledyard, Connecticut. As many as 20,000 people visit the casino on a single summer day. Many people come for a day of fun, leaving their homes in surrounding states early in the morning to arrive at Foxwoods by seven a.m. before the casino is so crowded that they have to wait to play their favorite games. Total bets run about $500,000 on a slow day, and on a busy weekend day as high as $3 million. The tribe pays the state of Connecticut a minimum of $100 million each year.[8]

Nationwide, American Indian casinos have become a multibillion-dollar-a-year industry, even though they control only a small percentage of the gambling activity in the United States. Tribes around the country have joined efforts to provide games that are relatively free of organized-crime infiltration, even though most of these tribes had little connection with each other in the past. However, there have been reports of criminal influence either directly through management and investment or indirectly through suppliers.[9]

ONE-ARMED BANDITS AND A DAY AT THE RACES

Slot machines are the most popular attractions at casinos. These "one-armed bandits" received their nickname from the lever the player pulls after dropping in a coin. Slots have been modernized with buttons, which makes the action move more quickly. Bright lights flash, spinning wheels hum, and symbols roll into place as the players wait and hope for the clang of the jackpot bells. Video slot machines and video poker machines offer fast-paced action and sophisticated computer graphics to attract players to the machines and to keep playing.

The games at all casinos are much the same: keno, bingo, craps, blackjack, and more. Players take their choice, but few remember that the casinos are built on the money the players lose. For most games, luck is more important than skill.

Luck is less important in horse betting because bets can be made based on information on the differ-

**Playing the "slots" at the Foxwoods Casino
in Connecticut. Notice that all the players
have to do is push a button to make the reels
spin, which allows for faster play—and
more money bet on each machine.**

ent horses and their riders. Handicapping means
predicting the outcome of a race based on this kind
of information, much of which is given in racing
forms, special newspapers popular among racing
enthusiasts.

When a bet is placed on a horse, the money becomes part of a betting pool, and each bet determines the ever-changing odds, that is, the relative chances of a loss or victory for each of the horses. Horse betting is a pari-mutuel, a system in which the winners divide the total amount bet after paying management expenses. As a bet is placed into the system, the totalizer, or "tote," automatically records it with other bets and sets the odds. Information that appears on the "tote board" at the tracks is determined by the number and the dollar amount of the bets, and is changed electronically about every ninety seconds while bets are being placed.

Betting can be done at the racetrack in most states, and in some states bettors can also place bets at offtrack and simulcast sites where they can watch the race live on television. They can also place bets by telephone.

The amount of money bet on horse racing decreased by the 1990s, possibly because of increased competition from other forms of legal gambling.

Betting on jai alai is legal in some states. Jai alai is a fast-paced game in which players hurl a ball against the front wall of a court, using a large curved basket strapped to their arms. The object of the game is to hurl the ball with so much speed and spin that the opponent cannot catch and return it on the fly or on the first bounce.

Dog races attract gamblers, too. Eight greyhounds in numbered stalls cry and yelp before the lever is pulled to open the gates. An electronically controlled "rabbit" incites the dogs as they run around the track. Some spectators think these races are more exciting than horse racing. Pari-mutuel betting on greyhounds is much the same as on horses, and a "tote board" displays the odds.

Legal in 37 states, as well as in Washington, D.C., state-run lotteries are among the most popular games today.[10] Choosing numbers is fun for some players. They select birthdays of family and friends, or other "lucky" numbers.

Multimillion-dollar jackpots excite television viewers from coast to coast, and many people who rarely buy a lottery ticket take a chance on the big ones. Some compulsive gamblers, who hope to get rich quick, might even bet the money they need for food and other necessities.

If people buy a large quantity of lottery tickets, they increase the chances of winning. No one ever receives the full amount of the ticket even when there is only one winning ticket. The federal government takes its share for taxes. State and local governments may take their share, too. Also, many states pay out only a fixed amount of the winnings each year and earn interest on the rest of the money.

Lotteries are popular because betting is easy, the tickets are not expensive, and the chance to win big is exciting. For some, the idea of contributing to a worthy cause, even if one does not win, is also a factor.

Some critics say that governments should not be in the gambling business at all.[11] There is some controversy about how much of the lottery income in different states actually goes to education or to the purposes that are advertised.

New Hampshire's lottery was introduced in 1963–1964 as a way of supporting schools without state income or sales tax revenues.[12] Other states

As lottery prizes grow larger, the lines to purchase tickets lengthen, even though the odds of winning can be more than a million to one.

followed New Hampshire, after cautiously waiting to see what effects state-supported gambling would have.

In 1967, New York State began its lottery. It has been projected by some that lotteries will be in all states by the end of the twentieth century.

The winning numbers for lotteries are selected slightly differently from state to state. Generally, numbered rubber or Ping-Pong balls are mixed in a machine and then drawn by being air-blown one by one into a separate compartment.

Can the lottery be fixed by weighting the balls? Some lottery employees tried this in 1980. They injected white latex paint into some of the balls to make them heavier. The employees were caught and jailed. Today, security arrangements are changed frequently, and periodically different people are chosen to supervise the drawings.[13]

Instant, or scratch-off, tickets are popular because players discover right away if they have won. Other popular games are Powerball, Lotto America, and Megabucks, which give players the chance to win huge jackpots. Some jackpots exceed $100 million. For these lotteries, a number of states pool funds to make huge jackpots. About $700 million was spent for multistate lottery tickets in 1993. One winner earned $111 million, the biggest return on a single winning lottery ticket in U.S. history.[14]

Bingo is another popular form of gambling. Bingo games are played in houses of worship, nursing homes, and retirement communities, where the social aspect of the game is emphasized. Played with cards that have five rows of five numbers, bingo offers various combinations of winning patterns, with names such as doghouse, chatterbox, golf club, and razor blade. The caller, who picks the numbers at random, tells the players which patterns or combinations will win before the game begins. Players cover each number as it is called if it appears on their cards. The first player to cover the winning combination gets the money.

Most bingo nights earn relatively small amounts for charities, but some involve large sums of money. For example, the Proctorsville, Vermont, fire department's bingo game has financed more than $700,000 in equipment and buildings. Entrance fees are as high as $100, and the prize may be as high as $16,000.[15] The largest bingo game in the country is held at Foxwoods, the casino run by the Mashantucket Pequot Indians in Connecticut.

Keno, a variation of bingo, is played in many casinos and state lotteries. The player gets a card with eighty numbers on it and marks from one to fifteen of the numbers. Twenty numbered balls are then selected by the casino. The player can win different amounts of money from even a small bet. The odds of winning are so heavily stacked against the keno player that it has been called a sucker's game.[16]

Sweepstakes contests mail announcements that huge sums of money will be paid to winners. The "winners" often find they have to buy something to win, or go through another drawing to be a final contest winner. These sweepstakes are used as a form of advertising for a wide variety of products. Commercial sweepstakes register with state governments and comply with strict state and federal laws; however, in some illegal sweepstakes, players are asked for money in the same letter that informs them they have won.

In all number games, luck determines the winner. Skill plays little or no part, and the odds of winning are incredibly low. With so many opportunities to gamble legally, one might assume that the popularity of illegal gambling has declined. It hasn't.

Chapter Four

Problems of Illegal Gambling

Back-room gambling existed long before legalized gambling arrived on the scene, and many "underground" clubs still exist throughout the nation. Illegal gambling houses have no controls. The players have no protection against cheating. One argument for legalizing gambling is to protect the players. For the millions who play illegally, the odds of losing are great.

Legal lotteries were supposed to eliminate the illegal numbers games, but "rackets" continue to thrive, especially in poor sections of large cities. According to some estimates, at least 20 million people a day contribute to the billions that are collected in numbers rings, certain that their lucky number will win.[1] Illegal bets on numbers range from a dime to $1,000 a day.

Betting parlors may be part of clothing stores, shoe stores, variety stores, candy stores, barbershops, or gas stations. Often, in a secluded part of the store, bets are recorded in triplicate on slips, showing the amount and the numbers selected. One copy is given to the customer; one is kept at the betting parlor. "Runners," or messengers, take the third slips to "policy banks" and the cash to "money banks." Clerks in the policy banks determine which bets are winners and the amounts to be paid out by the parlors.

Runners are at the bottom of the power ladder in the numbers organizations, with "bankers," operators, distributors, and agents each at different rungs. Each one gets a cut of the money. Runners and agents are often the most likely to be arrested, but higher-ups usually see that they are bailed out of jail.

"Hitting the numbers" is the expression for picking the right number between zero and 999. The odds against the player are so great that the numbers racket offers the best profits of any form of gambling.[2]

Organized crime controls many games, according to authorities.[3] Gangs and other groups may also control the numbers games in their "territories." Many murders have been committed over the years to gain control of or to hold on to numbers games.

GOVERNMENT CRACKS DOWN ON ILLEGAL GAMBLING NETWORKS

As stated previously, there have always been loose connections between criminals and gambling. As early as 1935, illegal gambling establishments criss-crossed the United States.[4] Corruption and gambling played a part in triggering the 1950 hearings of the Special Senate Committee to Investigate Crime in Interstate Commerce that was chaired by Senator Estes Kefauver of Tennessee. The committee called more than 450 witnesses and, among other things, it discovered that there was a well-organized network of illegal gambling operations that were protected by payoffs in many large cities. The network involved men who were connected with organized crime.[5] As a result of the hearings, federal and state crime commissions were formed to focus on curbing organized crime.

During the investigations, Senator Kefauver cited one gambling den as typical—the Last Chance Tavern in Kansas City, Missouri, located on the border between Missouri and Kansas, where a thin wall divided the action between one state and the other. Senator Kefauver described the operations as follows: When the police from Kansas arrived to "raid" the place, the gamblers quickly moved their equipment to the Missouri side of the building. When the Missouri police came, they moved to the state of Kansas. Since the police from each state never came at the same time, the racket worked and the tavern made a great deal of money.[6]

The government has investigated crooked gambling practices many times and passed laws that attempt to supervise gambling establishments, but according to David Oritz, author of *Gambling*

Scams, widespread corruption still exists in many illegal gambling houses.

There is also concern about illegal connections with legal gambling. In his book *Temples of Chance,* David Johnston says that the casino industry has passed from the hands of the old-style gangsters to the new generation of "respectable" business people. He says that the immense profit potential of the gambling business has sucked in corporation giants who have put large amounts of their resources into mega-casinos.

PIT BULLS AND COCKFIGHTING: ILLEGAL GAMBLING ACTION

Many types of illegal gambling common in the past exist today. Pit bulls are used in dogfights in which owners bet heavily on their own dogs. These dogs fight bloody battles, while observers bet among themselves and either with or against the owners as to which dog will win. Much negative publicity has been directed against dogfighting by people concerned about its cruelty. Local humane societies enlist the support of the public in their efforts to discourage this kind of "sport." Efforts are being made to catch the criminals who stage them and the spectators who bet on them.[7]

Cockfighting is another cruel, illegal sport that is popular with some gamblers and more common than dogfighting. Cockfighting was imported into

A cockfighting scene in Louisiana. Sometimes the roosters are fitted with steel spurs to add to the excitement and the gore.

the United States from the Caribbean islands and Mexico, where it has long been a part of the culture. Vacant buildings are turned into exhibition halls, and large amounts of money change hands. Local laws generally ban cockfighting, but the practice continues. Gambling rings sometimes secretly weaken one bird, so that it will be a sure loser.[8]

Gambling pools are a widespread form of illegal gambling. For example, someone may start a pool to bet on the date a baby will be born. Everyone who joins the pool contributes a dollar and makes a guess about the birth date, the sex, or the weight of the baby. Someone keeps a record of the bets and, when the baby arrives, gets all the correct information. The new mother may be pleased that her friends have shown such an interest in her baby. She does not know that the person who guesses the right date, sex, or weight wins a sum of money.

Although pools are illegal, they are also often a form of social activity. Most pools are for sporting events, and everyone contributes the same amount of money to the pot.

Illegal betting on horse and dog racing through bookmakers, or "bookies," still exists. The amount of money bet illegally on horse races is believed to be much greater than the amount bet legally. In many cases, the laws against such betting are only weakly enforced.[9]

Betting on other sports, such as football, basketball, and golf is usually illegal. Sports betting is legal in five states, but Nevada is the only state in which it is legal statewide. In Oregon, one can bet on certain sports by buying lottery tickets whose profits are intended to support college sports programs.[10] Delaware has authorized sports betting but has not carried it out. Sports betting takes place in limited localities in Montana and North Dakota.

Throughout the United States, more money is bet on football than any other sport. Many Americans, who consider themselves totally law-abiding, bet on the Super Bowl with the same holiday spirit in which they buy roses for Valentine's Day and turkey for Thanksgiving. Super Bowl Sunday has been called a betting extravaganza. The World Series and every other major sports event bring wagers of a wide variety.[11]

In Las Vegas, where sports betting is legal, sections of the casinos, which are called sports books, attract men and women who watch walls covered with color video screens and monitors that show games from all around the United States. The spectators bet on the games against the house.

In 1992 a federal law banned sports betting in any state that did not already have it, although New Jersey was allowed an extra year to seek to approve it because a sports betting bill had been introduced in the state's legislature in the summer of 1991. When the bill was debated in New Jersey, opponents raised moral and financial issues and the bill did not pass.[12]

The federal bill against sports betting was introduced because betting on games might corrupt athletes and the public and because it might encourage teen gambling. Even though legal sports betting is restricted to certain areas, everyone knows there is a tremendous amount of betting on football, baseball, basketball, hockey, golf, tennis, and other sports. The controversy over how much sports betting will spread to other states has cooled since the new legislation forbids it. Illegal bets are still made at social events and offices.

For many young people, sports betting is the beginning of an obsession that can sometimes lead to the need for membership in Gamblers Anonymous or activities that can result in an arrest record.

TWO REAL-LIFE CASES

Brad was only sixteen years old when he organized a sports betting business in his home. His parents were pleased that he spent so much time working on his computer, but they did not know how he was spending his time. Almost everyone at his high school did. His friends called with their bets, or even sent them by E-mail.

Brad had a thriving business until someone alerted the police. His operation closed, and he was arrested. But sports betting continued at his school and at many others.

Joe started to gamble seriously when he was attending high school in New Jersey. He distributed weekly football betting tickets to his schoolmates and he quickly built a clientele of about a hundred students. Although most of them lost money, Joe averaged about $250 a week from his gambling activities. After graduating from high school, he continued betting heavily in college. He would go to the store every morning to buy newspapers in order to check the day's betting lines and review statistics about teams. At first, he won big, but then his luck began to change.

One Sunday afternoon, Joe made a $3,000 bet on a football game and lost on the second touchdown. He felt he had no choice but to double his bet the next day to try to win his money back. He lost $7,000. Joe was able to pay the bookmaker from old winnings, but within a few weeks he had lost another $10,000. He was sure his luck would change so he tried to get his money back all at once by betting $10,000. His team lost. Now he owed the bookmaker $20,000. He had only the rest of the week to pay all he owed. If he could not, his bookie suggested that he borrow from a team of loan sharks linked with organized crime. Joe was afraid to borrow from them. He had heard they harassed people who could not pay and often threatened them physically until they did. Joe managed to borrow enough from a friend to bet $10,000 through another bookmaker. He won only that $10,000 back. He was still short $10,000.

Joe had no choice and finally told his parents how much he owed. They were very shocked and very disappointed. Rather than see him get into deeper trouble, they gave him $10,000 from their savings. Joe stopped betting—until the next football season. After more serious losses, his life was threatened by money collectors with connections to organized crime. Again, friends bailed him out. Joe knew he had gambled with more than money; he had gambled with his life. This time he stopped.[13]

Compulsive gamblers often desperately need money to continue gambling or to pay their debts.

Teenage gamblers have burglarized homes, shop-lifted, and sold drugs to pay off debts and gamble again. They "borrow" from their parents' wallets with every intention of repaying them. Many adults who have gambling problems have been known to write checks on accounts that do not have sufficient funds to cover them, forge checks, or even use money from their businesses. These and other thefts are usually not intended to hurt anyone, nor is there the fear of punishment. A gambler often does not consider the consequences when committing a crime to get money to gamble.[14] Although most people who commit crimes in order to get money to gamble were honest when they began to gamble, their increasing need for money and to continue gambling causes them to commit criminal activities. Gambling was called a "ticket to crime and corruption" at a recent meeting of attorneys general of six states.[15]

Gambling has become a very sophisticated activity, as noted on the book jacket of David Johnston's *Temples of Chance:* "Business school managers and skilled managers have replaced mob muscle, but casinos now rely on new forms of loaded dice—computer geniuses who carefully stack the odds, government officials who support corporation deal makers at the expense of the little guy, and subtle psychological techniques that invite addictive behavior."[16]

Chapter Five

Compulsive Gambling

Gambling has been called the addiction of the 1990s. Can you imagine a man robbing a bank with a water pistol to get money for gambling? Or can you picture a mother taking all the money saved for her daughter's college tuition so she could continue to gamble? For these people gambling changed from something they wanted to do to something they had to do. Getting the money to gamble became a need that was met by means that once they would not have dreamed possible. They needed to gamble.[1]

Compulsive gamblers have been known to act in many ways that are hard to believe. For example, a man who had bet heavily on the sex of the baby his wife was expecting was told he was the father of a boy. Later, he admitted to his therapist that he did not take the time to ask the obstetrician about the health of his wife or the baby. He rushed off to collect his winnings from a friend so he could pay his bookie some of the money he owed him from earlier gambling losses.

While gambling is a form of fun for most people, about 2 to 6 percent of the adult population in the United States have a serious problem with it.[2] Their gambling can result in financial ruin, loss of jobs, broken homes, criminal acts, physical illnesses, and suicide attempts. For them, gambling is as powerful as a drug addiction.

Not everyone agrees about the term that should be used to describe people who have serious problems with gambling. "Compulsive" is probably the most popular description for one whose gambling is out of control. Mental-health professionals prefer the term "pathological," since they consider such gambling an illness and the term pathological means "relating to disease." The American Psychiatric Association considers gambling a dependency that can be treated. Their *Diagnostic and Statistical Manual* describes a number of characteristics of dependency. One is a need to increase the amount and frequency of the behavior to achieve the desired excitement (also called tolerance). Other characteristics are discomfort on abstinence (withdrawal symptoms); impaired control of the behavior (or repeated failure to cut down or stop); and performance of the action more often than intended. Another characteristic is the activity's interference with health and social functioning. Compulsive gamblers have many of these problems.[3]

Players wait patiently to enter the world's largest bingo parlor in Florida. While for some, gambling may be only entertainment, for others it can be a form of compulsive behavior.

REASONS FOR
COMPULSIVE GAMBLING

Opinions vary as to why people become compulsive gamblers. The biology of the brain may hold the key to the problem.

Some people have symptoms similar to those in adults with attention deficit disorder, or hyperactivity. Individuals have been shown to have various levels of brain chemicals that regulate arousal, thrill, and excitement. Scientists have found high levels of norepinephrine and its breakdown products in the cerebrospinal fluid and urine of pathological gamblers. Norepinephrine is a hormone produced in the adrenal glands that has stimulating effects on the central nervous system. High-stakes gambling, which would make most people feel uncomfortable or very stressed, can make compulsive gamblers feel pleasantly alive.[4]

According to Arnold Wexler, Executive Director of the Council on Compulsive Gambling in New Jersey, compulsive gamblers feel the same sort of euphoria, or high, that is associated with drug addiction. The high is related to the release of endorphins, body chemicals that have a morphinelike, pain-relieving effect in the brain. Problem gamblers chase the high and need the experience much as drug addicts need their drug to feel normal. Like drug addicts, compulsive gamblers also experience withdrawal symptoms when they're not gambling.[5]

Many experts, including Valerie Lorenz, who is internationally known in the field, believe that compulsive gambling is a psychological addiction in which the abused substance is money. She believes compulsive gambling is a form of self-medication to escape depression, anxiety, and emotional discomfort. Gambling becomes a pleasure-seeking and pain-avoidance behavior, which is the hallmark of all addictions.[6]

Severe depression, anxiety disorders, and mental disorders characterized by unrestrained behavior are frequently associated with pathological gambling. Gambling problems are especially common among alcoholics and other drug abusers. In studies of teens who were hospitalized for drug abuse, 14 percent were pathological gamblers and another 14 percent had some problems with gambling.[7] Gamblers are more likely to be sociopaths than the average person. A sociopath does not live by the moral rules in society, does not learn from experience, lacks remorse, and shows poor judgment and little sense of responsibility.

These are just a few of the theories about why people gamble excessively, and several of these reasons may be involved in any one case. No matter what the cause, millions of people have uncontrollable urges and a compulsion to gamble. Their families often suffer long before they know what is wrong. The family may try to excuse some of the strange things that are happening, and often refuse to believe that the relative gambles uncontrollably. A compulsive gambler's absences from home, excuses, lies, and many personality changes are not the only difficulties for the family. There are also the many problems created by having less money to live on because of the gambling losses.

MAXIE: LIFE WITH A COMPULSIVE GAMBLER

The case that follows is based on one told by a therapist. Maxie (not her real name) is a girl whose father was a compulsive gambler. When Maxie was ten years old, she enjoyed going to the races with her father. Her mother always complained about these outings because her father lost so much money. Now and then he would win a large amount, and when that happened her mother would stop complaining for a while. She would tell herself, "Maybe he really will win big the next time." Maybe it was easier to think that way than to scold.

By the time Maxie was ready for high school, she knew that her father really had a gambling problem. She and her mother talked about it, but they did not know how to cope with it. One afternoon when Maxie was helping her mother fix dinner, they heard a crash of glass in the living room. They rushed to see what was happening. Her father's football team had lost in the last few seconds of the game. He had thrown her mother's favorite vase through the window. They watched as he banged his fist on the wall. Then he went upstairs and slammed the door of the bedroom.

Maxie and her mother went back to the kitchen and continued to cook dinner. They pretended that nothing had happened, but they both knew that there would be an empty place at the dinner table. They suspected that Maxie's father had lost a large amount of money on that football game. He had been losing so much money lately that her mother had threatened to take Maxie and go somewhere else to live. But she did not know where to go.

Life at home continued with one argument following another. Every morning, Maxie would wake up dreading the screaming that would surely start again.

This went on for a year, while her father continued to gamble heavily. The family's savings were gone; paychecks were lost. The heat and phone were shut off. There was never enough money for food and clothing. At times Maxie's grandmother bailed her son out of his gambling debts, because she believed his life was in danger. She also believed his promises to stop gambling.

Maxie's father always meant to keep his promises when he made them, but soon he would bet on something again because he was sure he was ready for the big win. He always planned to pay back all the people he owed. But whenever he won some money, he felt he was on a lucky streak and he gambled with his winnings until the money was gone.

Maxie's father had always been an honest man, but after gambling took over his life, he "borrowed" money from some accounts at his firm. He was sure he could return the money when his luck was better. Of course, he continued to lose money, and his "borrowing" was discovered. He was convicted of embezzlement and sent to jail. Even in jail, he gambled in his mind. Every morning, he read the sports column in the newspaper, picked out the most likely winners of the day's games, and waited anxiously for the results.

Maxie's mother felt angry and depressed. She often asked herself what went wrong with her marriage. Sometimes Maxie blamed herself for upsetting her father when she took sides with her mother in their arguments. She loved her father, but she hated going to the prison to see him. She despised all kinds of gambling. She tried to remember the old days when her father did not seem to have his awful gambling problem. She was embarrassed about her father's arrest. A few of her old friends avoided her, but she told herself that they were not true friends, for the friends most important to her seemed to understand.

A counselor at Maxie's school suggested that she attend meetings of Gam-A-Teen, an organization for teenagers that had been formed by family members and close friends affected by a loved one's gambling problems. Once Maxie started attending meetings, she wished she had known about the group sooner, for it helped her understand her father's problem and to learn how to deal with her feelings.

STAGES OF
COMPULSIVE GAMBLING

According to the late Dr. Robert Custer, an expert in the diagnosis and treatment of gambling disorders, there are three phases to becoming a compulsive gambler.[8] The first is the winning phase, where there are many small wins, some losses, and sometimes a big win. This makes the gambler prone to compulsive behavior feel important and confident, rather than fearful and depressed.

Many compulsive gamblers suffer from low self-esteem. They do not believe that they can do anything right, so they keep putting themselves down. They have not learned how to communicate effectively, and they do not have good coping skills. Gambling is a way to live in a different world. They feel better about themselves while they are gambling. They believe they will become more likable if they are winning money. As the gambling increases, they fantasize about winning lots of money and being a "big shot."

The second phase in the development of an addiction to gambling is losing. The bubble that carried these gamblers into a world of fantasy bursts, as the overall winning streak they enjoyed for a short time ends. The amounts of their bets have gradually grown. They started betting big money because they felt invincible. Now they must face reality. Their debts are big and their losses persist. They cover up their problem with lies, borrow small amounts, delay paying bills, and then begin to borrow more heavily.

At the third stage, desperation, compulsive gamblers no longer believe that they can conquer their problem. They are not propelled by the euphoria of winning, but they continue to gamble to win back some of their losses. They may borrow money illegally. They may write bad checks, resort to fraud, embezzlement, stealing, or just about anything to get the money to bet and stay in the action.[9] Gamblers call this "chasing," frantically pursuing lost money.

At some point, the compulsive gambler asks relatives to pay gambling debts. When this happens, the secret is out. The gambler may be relieved that his family knows about his problem, but he may also continue to gamble.

Gambling is no longer something compulsive gamblers want to do. It is something they must do. Many gambling addicts cannot stop on their own no matter how hard they try.[10] They need help.

Chapter Six

Young Gamblers

Pitching pennies, flipping for baseball cards, playing cards for money, betting on sports, or having an older friend buy a lottery ticket are some of the popular ways kids gamble to have fun. Not everyone who gambles will become a compulsive gambler, but for a small percentage, gambling becomes a serious problem. Sometimes families encourage gambling. This can lead to trouble without the family's even realizing it.

The Dunn family has fun gambling together. Mom, Dad, and the ten-year-old twins, Peter and Greg, go to the mall weekly, and while they are there Mr. Dunn buys four "pull tabs." These little cardboard tickets are sold at vending machines. Each family member pulls a ticket and peels back the paper slots to reveal the results. Usually, no one wins a prize, but each hopes for better luck next time. On Greg's birthday, he won a hundred dollars. The whole family said he was lucky because it was his

"Daddy took me to the zoo. One of the animals came
in and paid $33.80 across the board."

**A parent can easily make gambling
seem very appealing to an impressionable
child, thus passing an addiction along
to the next generation.**

birthday, but Peter complained that it was his birthday too, and he hadn't won anything. Peter decided
he wanted to be a winner and began using his
spending money to gamble with an older school
friend. This may, or may not, lead to a problem later,
for there are many factors involved, but the twins,
who are only ten years old, are breaking the law
when they gamble in any form.

For most gamblers, the fun of winning is the

thing that they remember, and not that the total amount they spent on gambling over a period of time was much greater than the hundred dollars that was won once.

Today's generation of young people is probably the first to be immersed in video technology as entertainment, on personal computers and in shopping-mall arcades. Few notice that the only skill required in these games is staying on the machine and in the action. Many adults are concerned about the large numbers of young people who have taken up video gambling as "harmless fun." Researchers say that addiction to gambling is growing fastest among high school and college students.[1]

Young compulsive gamblers are often bright, competitive, athletic, and hardworking. They may be shy and easily frustrated, have low self-esteem, get bored easily, and tend to hide their feelings. Most believe that money will solve their problems.[2]

JED: DICE AT SEVEN— CASINOS AT SEVENTEEN

Consider the case of Jed (not his real name), a teenager who spent many hours gambling in shopping-mall arcades. Jed had learned to gamble at the age of seven when his father tossed dice with him in an effort to teach him simple arithmetic. Through the years, Jed and his father enjoyed a number of differ-

The concentration of these teens on
the video games eerily mimics the
concentration of slots players at casinos.

ent gambling games together, and Jed noticed that his father seldom bothered with him unless gambling was involved. The games were fun, but the arguments that his mother and father had about the money that his father bet on the horses were not. They frightened Jed, and for good reason. Sometimes the arguments ended in violence.

By the time Jed became a teenager, his mother and father had separated, and Jed's father rarely came to see him. According to the custody agreement, Jed's father was permitted to spend every other weekend with his son, but he only came a few times in the year after the separation. He made excuses about not coming, and Jed soon learned that his father was too busy visiting the track and betting on the horses to take the time to visit his son. Instead of a birthday present from his father, there were apologies on the phone. His father promised he would soon win big and buy Jed whatever he wanted. But Jed knew he could not count on a present from his father.

For a few years, Jed hated all gambling. Then his friends began playing poker and craps. Jed could not resist showing them some of the things his father had taught him. They were too young to visit the casino, but they played craps every day after school. They played for small amounts of money, and the games were exciting for Jed, who won more often than he lost. He felt he was lucky, but he was careful to hide his afternoon games from his mother.

Gambling made Jed feel important, even though he could not spend his winnings for fear his mother would find out where he got the money. He waited eagerly for the completion of the new casino that was being built near his home. He decided he would save all of his winnings and make a trip to the new casino during opening week. He would join the

Young people study the racing forms at a New York racetrack. Besides being an illegal activity, gambling can be the beginning of a later addiction for some teens and children.

crowd who made regular trips to spend the morning or afternoon at the casino. Jed knew he was too young to be admitted, but he was confident he looked old enough to pass as an adult. And he had been sure to get a fake I.D. card.

The new casino near Jed's home was a small one that catered to serious gamblers. Although the owners planned to schedule rock concerts, pop singers, and other events, the main entertainment was gambling.

Jed wondered what the casino would look like inside. He had heard many casinos described as glitzy or glamorous. This one was not very fancy, and some of the construction work was still going on, but there were already plenty of slot machines, roulette wheels, baccarat and blackjack tables. There was even a sports bar where bettors could watch races taking place all over the United States. Jed thought he'd look around and maybe even gamble a bit.

As Jed walked through the doors of the casino with the crowd from the bus, he worried someone would discover his age. He had read about hidden security cameras, so he tried to act casual. No one questioned him. Soon he began to feel very pleased with himself about sneaking into a casino.

Jed wandered around the tables and listened to the sounds of the action. He watched the roulette wheels spin and the dice roll. He decided he felt confident enough to buy some chips from the cashier using the forged card for identification.

With the chips in his pocket, Jed stood behind the blackjack table, where the dealer shuffled the cards with ease. He noticed that the players looked very serious, even when winning, and even those who watched seemed to play along, applauding a win and moaning at a loss.

When one player quit and left the table, Jed hesitated and then took his place at the empty seat. He put some chips on the table and entered into the game, trying to appear cool. He had played blackjack with his friends many times, but this time he had to beat the dealer. People were watching as he bet, trying to get his cards to tally as close to twenty-one as he could. He lost on the first deal. His mouth was dry and his palms sweaty as the cards came off the deck. He lost again. Then he won. He felt his confidence return, and he stayed at the table until he had won a hundred dollars.

Jed cashed in his chips and considered the game to play next. He was fascinated by the clinking of coins as they dropped into the troughs at the bottom of the slot machines. Jed bought a roll of quarters and chose a slot machine that took multiple coins. He fed the machine quickly, gathering the coins that fell, putting some into a bucket, but most back in the machine.

Jed moved to another slot machine, but in less than an hour, he lost the hundred dollars he had won at blackjack and the money he had saved from his gambling at school. He spent the rest of the morning watching the players at the roulette table. As each

In the hope of attracting more gambling parents, many hotel casinos have added such elaborate attractions as circus acts or mini-theme parks designed to appeal to children.

ball spun and dropped into a slot with a number, he felt as excited or as disappointed as if he were playing himself.

Jed needed to get home before the end of the school day so his mother would not know he had not attended classes. On the bus ride home, Jed thought about his first day at the casino. He did not feel good at all. Jed thought about his father's love of gambling and the problems it caused his father and his family. He could understand his father better now, but understanding was not enough to make Jed stop.

Jed did not quit gambling. He lost more money and started to steal. He decided he had to ask for help. He made an appointment with the counselor at school. She said she would try to help him before he got so deeply involved that gambling became his way of life. The counselor spoke with Jed's mother, and together they convinced Jed to enter a treatment program especially for teens with addiction problems. Jed was one of the lucky ones.

PREVENTION PROGRAMS

In some places, young people are so concerned about teen gambling that they have begun to help each other. One outstanding example of this type of effort is the club at Pikesville High School, near Baltimore, Maryland. There, four boys—Ryan Cole, Michael Paul, Steven Epstein, and Marc Foreman—started a club called SAGA (Students Against Gambling Addiction). They saw many of their classmates flipping coins during study halls and between classes, and many were becoming seriously involved in gambling on cards and sports, losing hundreds of dollars. The four boys became aware of the problems of compulsive gambling through articles in the media so they started a club to promote awareness and pass along information about gambling addiction. News of the club spread throughout the school. Other students joined, stories appeared in the media, and adults helped support the group.

SAGA may spread to other schools, much the way SADD (Students Against Driving Drunk) did. It has the potential to help students nationwide to become aware of the problems of pathological gambling and to find better ways of having fun.[3]

Dr. Durand Jacobs, a psychologist and vice president of the National Council on Problem Gambling, states: "Little will change until society begins to view teenage gambling with the same alarm directed at alcohol and other drugs." Few states have educational programs that warn young people of the addictive side of gambling. Many kids and adults are unaware of it. Dr. Jacobs believes that one in ten high school students is experiencing gambling-related problems. Unless we wake up to the darker side of gambling, he warns, we are going to have a whole new generation lost to this addiction.

Young gamblers who realize that they are addicted can find help in a number of ways. More information on sources of help can be found at the end of this book.

Chapter Seven

Conflicting Views and the Future of Gambling

- Gambling is fun.
- Gambling is harmless.
- Gambling makes me feel alive.
- Gambling is addictive.
- Gambling can wreck lives.

All of these statements can be true. Only a small percentage of people who gamble become compulsive gamblers. Most people are social bettors, who have a predetermined amount of money that they are willing to lose and stop betting once they have lost it.

Many social gamblers may not know anyone who has a gambling problem. Elberta and her friends live in a retirement community. They seldom gamble, even among themselves, and when they do the stakes are not much more than a few dollars on a bridge game. Every year, Elberta and some friends meet to watch the Kentucky Derby. A few dollars are bet among this group of friends before they watch the race on television, sipping their mint juleps, the traditional Derby drink. They are excited about the beauty of the horses as they watch them run, but they also root loudly for their favorites to win. If social betting, betting among friends, is illegal in their state, they may not be aware of it. The excitement is great in Elberta's home that day and in other homes throughout the United States where people watch sports and bet together.

Elberta and her friends are enthusiastic about the possible introduction of more forms of gambling in their state. They are counting on the revenues from gambling to keep their taxes down. Voters are always looking for ways to raise revenues without resorting to a tax increase, and for some people gambling may be the answer. Others, however, are asking if gambling is really good for the state.

Many legislators have ethical reservations about raising money through gambling. When the government sponsors gambling, it sends a message to young people that gambling is harmless. Other critics of gambling say that advertising for state lotteries encourages people to gamble, and so government agencies should not be involved.

Imagine the excitement in New York State when the lottery jackpot reached a record $72.5 million on October 29, 1994. Long lines formed at the 8,000 ticket outlets, which, near the time of the drawing, sold as many as one million tickets in an hour as millions of people entertained high hopes for their bets. Chances of winning were 1 in 12.9 million, but four buyers shared the big prize.

The New York Lottery provided the state treasury with a billion dollars in each of two recent years.[1] No one knows how many of the ticket buyers could afford to spend money to take a chance on winning, but millions of faithful buyers continue to take their chances on a "dollar and a dream."

How much of the money spent on lottery tickets really goes to education, treatment of compulsive gamblers, and the charities that are supposedly being helped? It varies from state to state. Many states redirect money to their general funds. Some states decrease the amount that is earmarked for education in their budgets because they intend to use the revenue from the lottery as school funding. You can learn what happens to lottery money in your state by writing to your state lottery commission. Your librarian will be able to help you find the address.[2]

Some religious leaders criticize lotteries, which they believe perpetuate a quick-fix, something-for-nothing, get-rich-quick philosophy. The Reverend Joseph Lowry, President of the Southern Christian Leadership Conference in Atlanta, Georgia, says that lotteries send people a negative message about how to support charities.[3]

Another argument against the introduction of more gambling is that gambling tends to harm low-income people. Lotteries sell hope, and the poor often hope the most. When welfare checks are cashed for use at casinos or lottery ticket counters, many families do not have the money they need for food and rent.[4] Still another argument holds that gambling is a ticket to crime. High crime rates have been reported in popular gambling meccas, such as Atlantic City and Las Vegas.[5]

Many critics say that early promises of jobs and more money for local businesses remain unfulfilled

This cartoon shows a woman who has given in to the fantasy of sudden, effortless wealth— a fantasy she enjoys even while her real life is destroyed by her gambling addiction.

after casinos and other gambling operations open. Gambling's record of stimulating local economies is mixed, however. But in the small town of Tunica, Mississippi, riverboat gambling created 13,000 new jobs in two years and a tremendous expansion in investment in hotels, restaurants, and other businesses.

States and cities that hope to reap riches from gambling could be in for some unpleasant surprises, however, according to Robert Goodman, a professor of regional planning at the University of Massachusetts. Professor Goodman studies the effects of gambling as a government revenue source. He says that gambling often attracts more local residents than tourists, and this results in money being spent on gambling rather than on cars, clothing, and other items offered by community businesses.[6]

Many casinos have had increases in earnings, but critics claim that the money spent on gambling could be of greater benefit to the community if spent on different types of products. Casino investors earn their money back in a short time, but the costs to the communities are often hidden and long-term. For example, in addition to the human cost of compulsive gambling, there are the costs resulting from such problems as embezzlement, fraud, loss of productivity, extra policing, and alcohol-related accidents. According to Professor Earl Grinois, an economist at the University of Illinois, and other economists, the introduction of gambling can have economic costs that far outweigh the benefits.[7]

**Only a few blocks from the casinos of
Atlantic City, houses remain boarded up and
lots stay vacant as the hoped-for renewal
of the city continues to be elusive.**

Many states compete with one another for gambling dollars. When gambling is not available in one state, people travel to a state nearby and spend their money on games there. So many governments introduce gambling in their own states hoping to keep that money at home.

Gambling has also been called the "new buffalo" for American Indian groups. Much as the buffalo provided sustenance for some tribes long ago, gambling profits are providing large amounts of money for certain tribes today, helping them to build schools, health centers, and housing for the elderly. But there is another side to the picture. Some American Indians object to gambling, for, in their opinion, it takes away an individual's purpose, identity, heritage, and dignity. When only luck is involved, they believe, there is no grace to the human spirit. So even where gambling brings prosperity, there is controversy about its value.[8]

NEW TECHNOLOGY
AND GAMBLING

There is much controversy over the introduction of interactive gambling, in which electronic technology enables players to use television remote-control buttons to place bets. But that is just the beginning. Imagine the following scene that might take place as early as the year 2000:

Ben is a college student who loves to gamble, and he is excited about the new home-gambling network that uses interactive television. Now he can bet on sporting events, beauty contests, lotteries to win cash or credit for merchandise, and a wide variety of other events without leaving home. He can bet on which football team will score first, the distance of a golfer's drive on the eighth hole, or how many minutes it will take his favorite basketball team to score ten points.

When he plays on the home-gambling network, Ben can issue a lottery ticket to himself. He can call the betting agency on the phone, and a computer places his bet and runs a credit check. The money will be deducted from his bank account or charged to his telephone bill. A small printer, which has been installed next to his phone, issues the ticket. He uses a toll-free number, so his only charge is the amount he pays for his ticket.

The patent for interactive television gambling was issued in 1994.[9] It can include in-flight gambling programs on airplanes to win frequent-flier coupons, and gambling programs shown in hotel rooms, in casinos, and on riverboats. Players can gamble while propped up in bed.

Many of the problems connected with interactive television gambling have to be worked out, and cooperation will be needed among broadcast companies, sports teams, racetracks, banks, and telephone companies.

Questions remain about the negative side of a gambling network, even if it is run without any corruption. How will children be prevented from gambling? Will interactive television gambling encourage more gambling and an increase in the number of compulsive gamblers? Will people who cannot afford to bet do so anyway?

Do you think this kind of interactive betting should be legal in your state? Some people think it would be a fun addition to the many legal varieties that already exist. Others, who have studied the pros and cons of gambling, say that a society in which everyone dreams of becoming an instant millionaire creates a society of losers.

As voters consider adding new kinds of gambling to those that are already legal, is it time to re-examine the pros and cons of the whole situation? Will more opportunities for gambling create new and greater problems?

Help for Compulsive Gamblers

Do you have a friend who has a gambling problem? Perhaps you think you have a problem.

Gamblers are usually the last people to realize their own problems. Friends and family can offer support and information, but they cannot stop addictive behavior.

There are two kinds of professional programs to help gamblers. In one, patients live at the treatment centers; in the other, patients live at home and meet therapists at appointed times. All programs are confidential and provide the help needed to overcome gambling addiction.

Gamblers Anonymous is a worldwide nonprofit fellowship. There are no mandatory dues or fees, and anyone who is seeking help for a gambling problem is welcome. For more information about Gamblers Anonymous meetings in your area, consult your local telephone directory or write to the International Service Office listed on the next page.

Other sources of help are local addiction clinics, your state department of health, or a community mental-health center.

Gam-Anon and Gam-A-Teen help families of compulsive gamblers. You may find that there is a local chapter listed in your phone book.

Gamblers Anonymous
International Service Office, Inc.
P.O. Box 17173
Los Angeles, CA 90017
213-386-8789

Gam-Anon and Gam-A-Teen
P.O. Box 157
Whitestone, Queens, New York 11357
718-352-1671

NATIONAL HOTLINES

1-800-732-9808
(South Oaks Hospital,
Amityville, New York)

1-800-GAMBLERS
(New Jersey Council on
    Compulsive Gambling)

Notes

Chapter One

1. Valerie Lorenz, "An Overview of Gambling and Compulsive Gambling" (Baltimore: Compulsive Gambling Center, Inc., 1992), p. 3.
2. *U.S. News and World Report,* March 14, 1994, p. 43.
3. *Newsweek,* June 13, 1994, p. 44.
4. *New York Times,* August 2, 1990.
5. *Ibid.,* November 13, 1993.
6. Bertha Davis, *Gambling in America* (New York: Franklin Watts, 1992), p. 57.
7. *Christian Science Monitor,* October 8, 1993.
8. *Ibid,* January 26, 1993.
9. Carl Sifakis, *Encyclopedia of Gambling* (New York: Facts on File, 1990), p. 77.
10. *New York Times,* December 2, 1993.
11. David Spanier, *Easy Money: Inside the Gambler's Mind* (New York: Penguin Books, 1988), p. 140.
12. *New York Times,* August 29, 1993.

Chapter Two

1. A. J. Berger and Nancy Bruning, *Lady Luck's Companion* (New York: Harper and Row, 1979), p. 1.
2. John Scarne, *Scarne's New Complete Guide to Gambling* (New York: Simon and Schuster, 1974), p. 32.
3. Time-Life Editors, *A World of Luck: Library of Curious and Unusual Facts* (Alexandria, VA: Time-Life Books, 1991), p. 8.
4. Ralph Tegtmeier, *Casinos* (New York: The Vendome Press, 1989), pp. 15–16.
5. Alice Fleming, *Something for Nothing: A History of Gambling* (New York: Delacorte Press, 1978), p. 2.
6. *Ibid.*, p. 2.
7. *Ibid.*, p. 12.
8. Tegtmeier, p. 18.
9. The Bible, Proverbs 16:33.
10. The Bible, Jonah 1:7.
11. Time-Life Editors, p. 11.
12. *Ibid.*
13. Berger and Bruning, p. 12.
14. *Ibid.*, p. 13.
15. Time-Life Editors, p. 10.
16. Fleming, p. 43.
17. Carl Sifakis, *Encyclopedia of Gambling* (New York: Facts on File, 1990), p. 187.
18. Fleming, pp. 59–60.
19. Scarne, p. 150.
20. Fleming, pp. 132–133.
21. Scarne, p. 33.
22. Sifakis, p. 199.
23. Mark Siegal et al., editors, *Gambling: Crime or Recreation* (Wylie, TX: Information Plus, 1992), p. 4.
24. *Ibid.*, pp. 4–5.
25. *Ibid.*, p. 5.

26. Fleming, p. 133.
27. *New York Times,* December 5, 1993.
28. *Christian Science Monitor,* January 26, 1993.

Chapter Three

1. *Christian Science Monitor,* January 23, 1993.
2. Bertha Davis, *Gambling in America* (New York: Franklin Watts, 1992), p. 20.
3. Ralph Tegtmeier, *Casinos* (New York: The Vendome Press, 1989), p. 140.
4. *Ibid.,* p. 142.
5. Davis, p. 23.
6. Mark Siegal, *Gambling: Crime or Recreation* (Wylie, TX: Information Plus, 1992), p. 37.
7. *New York Times,* April 10, 1994.
8. *Ibid.,* August 8, 1994.
9. *Christian Science Monitor,* May 23, 1994.
10. *New York Times,* December 2, 1993.
11. *Christian Science Monitor,* August 16, 1993.
12. Davis, p. 41.
13. Ben Johnson, *The Lottery Book* (New York: Avon Books, 1992), p. 29.
14. *U.S. News and World Report,* July 19, 1993, p. 17; Iowa Lottery Championship Year, 1993, p. 5.
15. *Burlington Free Press,* September 22, 1992.
16. Carl Sifakis, *Encyclopedia of Gambling* (New York: Facts on File, 1990), p. 174.

Chapter Four

1. Carl Sifakis, *Encyclopedia of Gambling* (New York: Facts on File, 1990), p. 209.
2. *Ibid.,* p. 210.
3. *Ibid.*

4. Ralph Tegtmeier, *Casinos* (New York: The Vendome Press, 1989), p. 139.
5. Alice Fleming, *Something for Nothing: A History of Gambling* (New York, Delacorte Press, 1978), p. 138.
6. Sifakis, pp. 183–184.
7. *Ibid.,* pp. 95–96.
8. *Ibid.,* p. 69.
9. Bertha Davis, *Gambling in America* (New York: Franklin Watts, 1992), pp. 54–57.
10. *Ibid.,* p. 43.
11. *Newsweek,* January 27, 1992.
12. *New York Times,* January 1, 1994.
13. *Paramus Sunday Record,* May 23, 1993.
14. Linda Berman and Mary-Ellen Siegal, *Behind the 8 Ball* (New York: Simon and Schuster, 1992), pp. 121–123.
15. *Boston Globe,* November 23, 1993.
16. David Johnston, *Temples of Chance: How America Inc. Bought Out Murder Inc. to Win Control of the Casino Business* (New York: Doubleday, 1992), jacket.

Chapter Five

1. "Compulsive Gambling," Compulsive Gambling Center, Baltimore, leaflet.
2. Jane Haubrich-Casperson, *Coping with Teen Gambling* (New York: Rosen, 1993), p. 118.
3. American Psychiatric Association, *Diagnostic and Statistical Manual,* IV, pp. 615–618.
4. Harvard Medical School, "Harvard Mental Health Letter," February 1992, p. 4.
5. Arnold Wexler, Article in *New View,* Newsletter of the Texas Commission on Alcohol and Drug Abuse, September 1993.
6. Valerie C. Lorenz, "An Overview of Gambling and Compulsive Gambling" (Baltimore: Compulsive Gambling Center, Inc., 1992), p. 6.

7. Harvard Medical School, "Harvard Mental Health Letter," February 1992, p. 5.
8. Robert Custer and Harry Milt, *When Luck Runs Out: Help for Compulsive Gamblers and Their Families* (New York: Facts on File, 1965), pp. 105–112.
9. Valerie C. Lorenz, "Compulsive Gambling" (Baltimore: Compulsive Gambling Center, Inc., 1992), booklet.
10. Valerie C. Lorenz, "Teen Gamblers," (Baltimore: Compulsive Gambling Center, Inc., 1992), booklet.

Chapter Six

1. *Christian Science Monitor,* May 23, 1994.
2. Valerie Lorenz, "Teen Gamblers," (Baltimore: Compulsive Gambling Center, Inc., 1992), booklet.
3. Ryan Cole, "Students Against Gambling Addiction," personal letter, September 13, 1994.

Chapter Seven

1. *New York Times,* October 31, 1994.
2. *Christian Science Monitor,* August 16, 1993.
3. *Ibid.*
4. *Ibid.,* January 25, 1993.
5. *Ibid.,* May 23, 1994.
6. *Ibid.,* August 8, 1994.
7. *New York Times,* June 12, 1994.
8. *Christian Science Monitor,* November 15, 1993.
9. *New York Times,* February 28, 1994.

Suggestions for Further Reading

Berman, Linda, and Mary-Ellen Siegal. *Behind the 8 Ball: A Guide for Families of Gamblers.* New York: Simon and Schuster, 1992.

Clotfelter, Charles, and Philip J. Cook. *Selling Hope: State Lotteries in America.* Cambridge, MA: Harvard University Press, 1989.

Custer, Robert, and Harry Milt. *When Luck Runs Out: Help for Compulsive Gamblers and Their Families.* New York: Facts on File, 1985.

Davis, Bertha. *Gambling in America.* New York: Franklin Watts, 1992.

Devol, George H. *Forty Years a Gambler on the Mississippi.* New York: Holt, 1926.

Haubrich-Casperson, Jane. *Coping with Teen Gambling.* New York: Rosen, 1993.

Heineman, Mary. "When Someone You Love Gambles." Center City, MN: Hazelden, 1993.

Heineman, Mary, "Losing Your Shirt." Minneapolis: CompCare, 1992.

Johnson, Ben. *The Lottery Book: Everything You Need to Know About the Big Money Games People Win Every Day*. New York: Avon Books, 1991.

Johnston, David. *Temples of Chance: How America Inc. Bought Out Murder Inc. to Win Control of the Casino Business*. New York: Doubleday, 1992.

Krantz, Les. *What the Odds Are*. New York: HarperCollins, 1992.

Lesieur, Henry. "Understanding Compulsive Gambling." Center City, MN: Hazelden, 1993.

Lorenz, Valerie C. "An Overview: Gambling and Compulsive Gambling." Baltimore: Compulsive Gambling Center, Inc., 1992.

Lorenz, Valerie C. "Releasing Guilt About Gambling." Center City, MN: Hazelden, 1993.

Manteris, Art. *SuperBookie: Inside Las Vegas Sports Gambling*. Chicago: Contemporary Books, 1991.

Ortiz, Darwin. *Gambling Scams.* New York: Dodd, Mead, 1984.

Siegal, Mark, et al., editors. *Gambling: Crime or Recreation*. Wylie, TX: Information Plus, 1992.

Sifakis, Carl. *Encyclopedia of Gambling*. New York: Facts on File, 1990.

Tegtmeier, Ralph. *Casinos*. New York: The Vendome Press, 1989.

Time-Life Editors. *A World of Luck: Library of Curious and Unusual Facts*. Alexandria, VA: Time-Life Books, 1991.

Walker, Michael B. *The Psychology of Gambling*. New York: Pergamon Press, 1992.

Glossary

Action: (1) Term used by gamblers to describe the excitement of betting. (2) Term used by gamblers to describe betting.

Bank: Person in charge of money at any gambling game.

Bingo: Game in which players must cover a pattern of numbers printed on a card using numbers randomly announced by a caller.

Blackjack: Popular card game in which the object is to be dealt cards whose numerical value comes as close as possible to 21 without going over that figure. The bettor plays against the dealer, or house.

Bookmaker: Person who accepts bets from gamblers. Also called a Book or Bookie.

Chasing: Gambler's attempt to break even, or win back money lost previously, by betting even more money.

Collector: Person employed by a bookie to collect money owed or to pay off winning bets.

Craps: Gambling game based on the roll of dice.

Hot: Descriptive of a gambler on a winning streak.

Hit: In blackjack, to ask for an additional card in an attempt to reach, or get as close as possible to, 21.

Jackpot: The top prize.

Jai Alai: Game played on an enclosed court, somewhat like squash, on which betting is permitted.

Keno: A game based on randomly chosen numbers, out of a field of up to eighty, selected by the player. Winnings are based on the correct numbers chosen. This game can be played on paper or on a video screen, and is often run by state lotteries or casinos.

Limit: Predetermined amount that can be wagered, usually in card games.

Lottery: (1) Contest in which players purchase tickets with anywhere from three to six numbers on them. Winning numbers are picked at random. (2) Contest in which players purchase tickets with preprinted numbers on them. The numbers are revealed by scratching off an ink covering or pulling open the tickets (see Pull Tab).

Number: (1) Amount of money won, lost, or owed. (2) Refers to an illegal numbers (lottery) game.

Odds: The probability of one thing happening rather than another.

One-armed Bandit: Slot machine.

Pari-mutuel: Type of gambling such as horse racing or bingo, where all the bets are combined in a pool; winners are paid off according to the number of winners in that pool.

Point Spread: Used in sports betting to give points to a team to even out the odds.

Poker Machine: A video-gambling device for playing poker or other games.

Pull Tab: Tab in slot of a paper or cardboard game of chance that is pulled open to reveal winning or losing combinations.

Raffle: A lottery.

Regressive Tax: Tax system in which low-income persons pay proportionately more tax relative to income than high-income persons.

Runner: see Collector.

Score: Big gambling win.

Spread: see Point Spread.

Stakes: Money or property risked in a bet or gambling game.

Twenty-one: Blackjack.

Video Slots: Electronic or computerized gambling games using a video-screen format.

Index

Norepinephrine, 55
Numbers games, 13, 42–43

Offtrack betting, 13, 26, 36
Oritz, David, 44

Pari-mutuel betting, 36, 37
Pathological gambling (*see* Compulsive gambling)
Paul, Michael, 71–72
Pools, 46–47
Prevention programs, 71–72
Professional gamblers, 24

Reform movements, 24–26
Regressive tax, 13
Reno, Nevada, 29
Riverboat gambling, 10, 24, 77
Romans, 20–21
Rose, Nelson, 12

SAGA (Students Against Gambling Addiction), 71–72
Self-esteem, 60, 64
Siegel, Benjamin (Bugsy), 27–28
Slot machines, 26, 34, *35*, 69
Social betting, 73–74
Sports betting, 10, 15, 47–50
Sweepstakes, 40–41

Teen gambling, 9, 15, 49–51, 56, 62–72, *65*, *67*
Tolerance, 55
Totalizer ("tote"), 36
Tunica, Mississippi, 77

Video games, 13, 34, 64, *65*

Washington, George, 23
Wexler, Arnold, 55
Withdrawal symptoms, 55